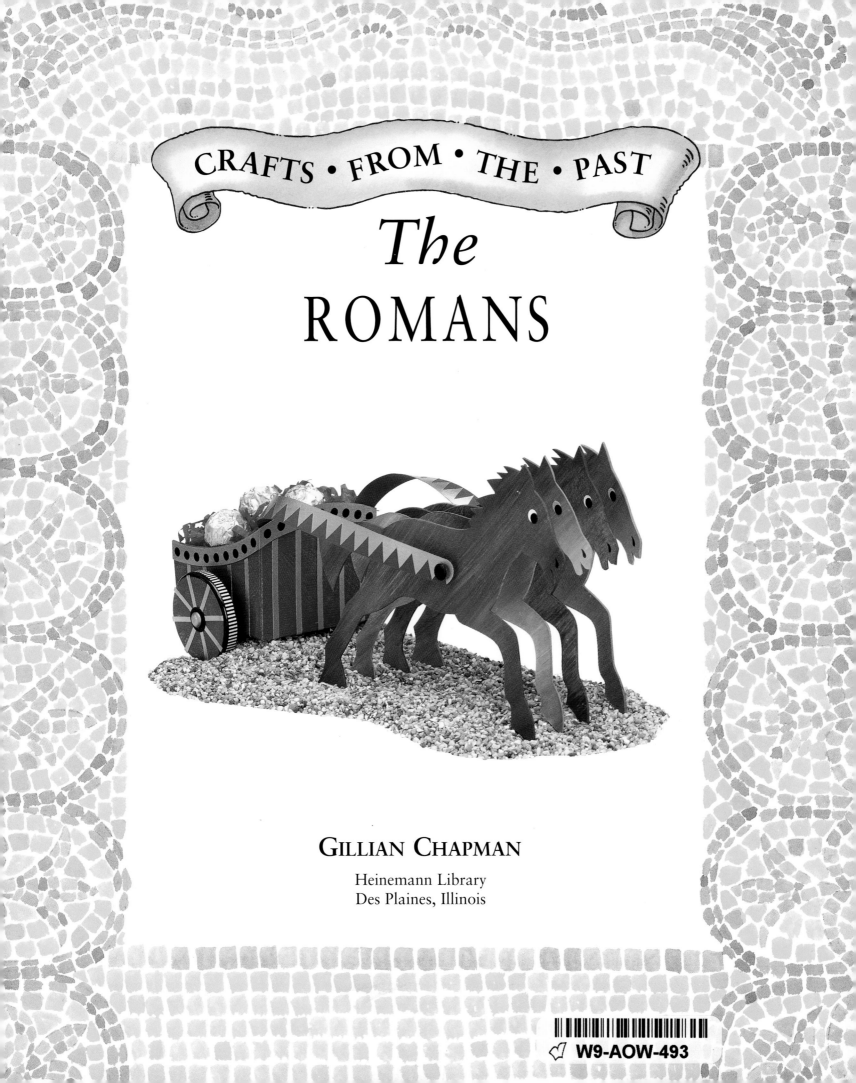

CRAFTS · FROM · THE · PAST

The ROMANS

GILLIAN CHAPMAN

Heinemann Library
Des Plaines, Illinois

General Craft Tips and Safety Precautions

Read the instructions carefully, then gather everything you'll need
before you begin to work.

It will help if you plan your design first on scrap paper.

If you are working with papier-mâché or paint, cover the work surfaces
with newspaper.

Always use a cutting mat when cutting with a mat knife and ask
an adult to help if you are using sharp tools.

Keep paint and glue brushes separate and always wash them out after use.
Use non-toxic paints and glue.

Don't be impatient—make sure plaster is set, and papier-mâché or paint
is thoroughly dry before moving on to the next step!

All the projects make perfect presents!
Try to make them as carefully as you can.

Recycling

Start collecting materials for craftwork. Save newspaper, colored
paper and cardboard, cardboard boxes and tubes of different sizes, magazines,
gift wrap, and scraps of string and ribbon.

Clean plastic containers and old utensils are perfect for mixing
plaster and making paper pulp.

Picture Credits

AKG Photos: 26; **British Museum:** 10, 16, 24, 34; **C.M. Dixon:** 6 bottom right, 8 top right, 12, 14, 22;
e.t. archive: 28; **Michael Holford:** 6 bottom left, 7 bottom left and right, 8 bottom right, 32;
Robert Harding: /Roy Rainford: 7 top left; **SCALA:** 8 bottom left; **Werner Forman Archive:**
/Museo Nazionale Romano, Rome 6 top left, 18, 20, 30, 36.

©1998 Reed Educational & Professional Publishing
Published by Heinemann Library,
an imprint of Reed Educational & Professional Publishing,
1350 East Touhy Avenue, Suite 240 West
Des Plaines, IL 60018

Produced by Fernleigh Books
Designers: Gillian Chapman and Gail Rose
Photographer: Rupert Horrox
Illustrator: Teri Gower Picture Researcher: Jennie Karrach
© Fernleigh Books 1998
Printed in Italy.

03 02 01 00 99 98
10 9 8 7 6 5 4 3 2 1

The author and Fernleigh would like to thank the following:
Keith Chapman for all his help with the model making.

Library of Congress Cataloging-in-Publication Data
Chapman, Gillian.
     The Romans / Gillian Chapman.
         p.   cm. — (Crafts from the past)
     Includes bibliographical references and index.
     Summary: Describes various aspects of life in ancient Rome and
provides instructions for creating related crafts, including
scrolls, temples, statues, and terracotta lamps.
     ISBN 1-57572-734-X (lib. bdg.)
     1. Handicraft—Rome—Juvenile literature.   2. Rome--Civilization-
-Juvenile literature.   [1. Rome—Civilization   2. Handicraft.]
I. Title.   II. Series.
TT16.C48   1998
937—dc21   98-15666
                                                                   CIP
                                                                   AC

Acknowledgments
Every effort has been made to contact copyright holders of any material
reproduced in this book. Any omissions will be rectified in subsequent printings
if notice is given to the publisher.

Some words are shown in bold, **like this**.
You can find out what they mean by looking in the glossary.

CRAFTS · FROM · THE · PAST

The ROMANS

GILLIAN CHAPMAN

THE ROMAN EMPIRE

ABOVE. *Roman soldiers in battle*

BELOW. *The Roman **Forum** was the seat of government.*

IN THE EIGHTH CENTURY B.C., Rome was a small farming community situated on seven hills overlooking the Tiber River. It soon developed into one of the most powerful cities of all time. At first the small town of Rome was governed by the **Etruscans** who ruled over central Italy, but noble Roman families overpowered the Etruscan kings and set up their own form of elected government. This marked the beginning of the Roman Republic in 509 B.C.

The descendants of these noble families, known as **patricians**, continued to rule Rome as **senators** and elected politicians for hundreds of years until the Republic fell into civil war. Eventually, a new system of rule and order was restored with an emperor in control. **Augustus** was the first Roman emperor and Rome was ruled peacefully by a succession of **emperors** for the next 400 years.

ABOVE. ***Augustus** ruled Rome from 27 B.C. to A.D. 14.*

THE POWER OF THE EMPIRE

ABOVE. *A Roman temple in Nimes, France*

BELOW: *The Pont du Gard, a Roman **aqueduct,** in Provence, France. It was three-stories high!*

THE ROMAN EMPIRE stretched over most of Europe, **Asia Minor,** and North Africa. It was linked by a network of roads, bridges, and **aqueducts.** After the army had conquered an area, the Romans would install a governor to keep the peace. Although they respected the customs of the people, the Romans were quick to leave their mark. They instigated huge building projects throughout the empire using local people as slave labor.

Roman architects and engineers were greatly influenced by Greek architecture, but they wanted to build bigger and better buildings. They used concrete, which was less costly and more versatile than stone, to build impressive structures. These were then covered with brick, plaster, or marble.

BELOW. *The ruined **Colosseum** in Rome was built for **gladiator** fights.*

ROMAN CULTURE

THE ROMANS admired Greek culture. All Roman art, sculpture, and literature shows the influence of the Greeks, but the Romans had a very different character. The Romans admired **"gravitas,"** which means strength and dignity, and perfectly describes the Roman personality. They portrayed themselves in a serious, dignified style.

Despite this portrayal of noble dignitaries, much of Roman society, especially business and politics, was corrupt and led by ambitious **emperors** who wasted public funds on huge **amphitheaters** and **circuses.** During the third century A.D. Roman generals began competing for power. Civil war, together with invasions along its vast borders caused the Empire to decline. In A.D. 324, the Emperor Constantine built a new capital at Byzantium, renaming it Constantinople. This led to further division within the Empire and the eventual fall of Rome.

*ABOVE. This statue of a **senator** shows the typical serious Roman style of sculpture.*

*BELOW RIGHT. Coin of Nero, one of the most corrupt of the Roman **Emperors.** He murdered his mother and his wife.*

*BELOW. Marble **relief** of chariot racing at the **Circus Maximus***

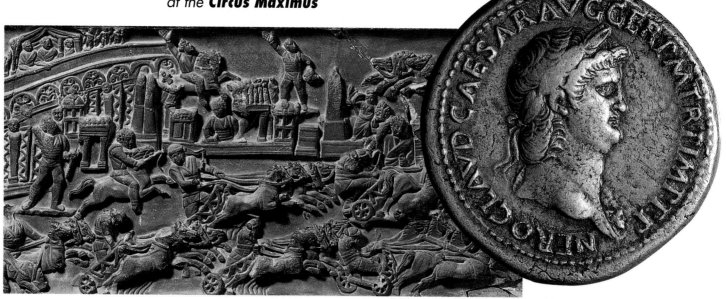

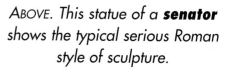

ROMAN CRAFT TIPS

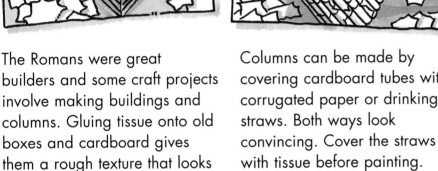

The Romans were great builders and some craft projects involve making buildings and columns. Gluing tissue onto old boxes and cardboard gives them a rough texture that looks like stonework.

Columns can be made by covering cardboard tubes with corrugated paper or drinking straws. Both ways look convincing. Cover the straws with tissue before painting.

Paint columns and buildings to look like marble or stone. Dab on thick gray and beige paint with a large brush. Don't forget to paint on some cracks and pieces of ivy.

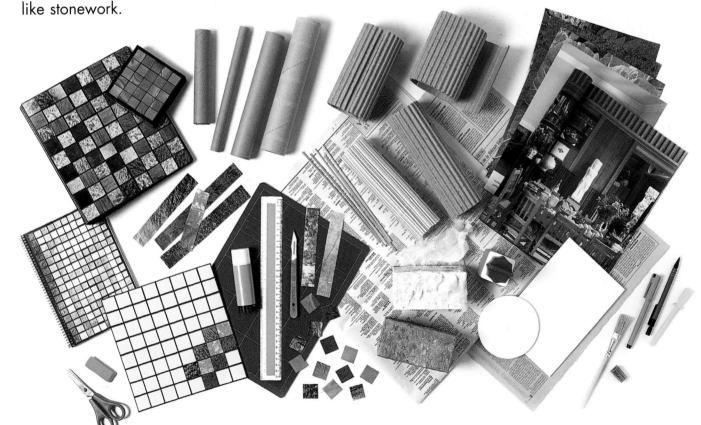

The Romans decorated their homes with mosaics and so can you. First draw a grid of squares with a black felt tip pen. Then color in the squares with felt tip pens or by gluing squares of colored paper.

Collect old magazines and cut out mosaic squares from the pages. It is an inexpensive and easy way of finding all the colors you need for your mosaic picture. Glue the squares down with a glue stick.

Some projects suggest using thick cardboard as a base or for part of the structure. Try using foam board instead. It is easy to buy from craft stores and is much easier to cut and shape than thick cardboard.

9

MAKING MOSAICS

THE ROMANS made spectacular mosaic pictures from small pieces of stone, or "**tesserae.**" Craftspeople laid colored cubes of white chalk, **terra-cotta**, blue or black slate, and yellow sandstone into wet cement.

Mosaics were used extensively to pave public buildings, but only the rich could afford them in their **villas**. Mosaic factories in Italy and **Gaul** produced catalogs of their designs ranging from inexpensive border patterns to very costly scenes from literature and **mythology**.

Many Roman mosaics are in perfect condition today, like the patterned floor panel above, that was made in A.D. 100.

BORDER PATTERNS

YOU WILL NEED

Graph paper or white paper, ruler & black felt tip pen
Felt tip pens
Scissors

Glue stick
Magazine pictures (for mosaic work)
Empty cardboard boxes to decorate

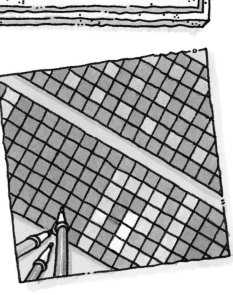

1. Use either the graph paper to design your mosaic patterns or draw your own grid by dividing white paper into 1/4 in. (1 cm) squares.

2. Cut a 1 1/2 in. x 1 1/2 in. (4 cm x 30 cm) strip of graph paper and make a two-color pattern by coloring in alternate squares. Make simple step designs.

3. Try making up your own designs using wider strips of paper with 3 or 4 colors. The designs shown above are often used in Roman mosaics.

Dress up old folders and notebooks with mosaic covers.

Use natural colors in your mosaic designs and transform cardboard boxes into stunning mosaic gift boxes.

SQUARE DESIGNS

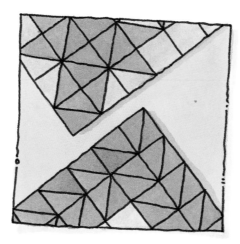

1. Cut out a grid measuring 2 in. (5cm) square and experiment with different designs. How many different patterns can you make?

2. Try using squares of different sizes. Divide the small squares in half to form triangles and include these in the design to make these "arrow" patterns.

3. Cut up colored paper into 1/4 in. (1 cm squares) and following your color scheme, glue them to your design for a really bold mosaic effect!

MOSAIC GAMES

SOME WEALTHY FAMILIES had baths in their homes, but most Romans went to the public baths to relax. The Romans loved to play games and the baths were an important place to exercise and socialize. Some men played ball games, wrestled, or trained with weights, while others preferred less energetic games. They sat with friends enjoying a board game or gambling with dice.

The modern game of Parcheesi is also known as Ludo. It takes its name from the Latin word "ludi" meaning game. Use mosaic patterns to decorate these Roman board games.

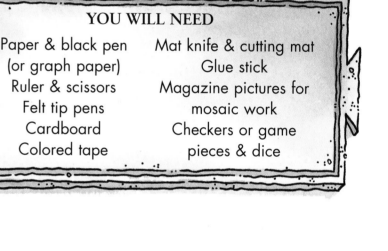

YOU WILL NEED

Paper & black pen (or graph paper)	Mat knife & cutting mat
Ruler & scissors	Glue stick
Felt tip pens	Magazine pictures for mosaic work
Cardboard	Checkers or game pieces & dice
Colored tape	

CHECKERBOARD

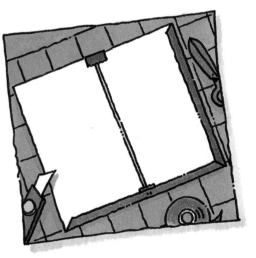

1. First you will need to plan the board design on paper. The checkerboard has eight squares on each side, plus a border. Plan out the measurements accurately.

2. Measure the size of the board design. Cut out a square of cardboard so when the board design is placed on top there is a 1/4 in. (1cm) gap left all around the edge.

3. Cut the cardboard square in half. Tape the two halves together, so the board can be folded. Tape the sides of the board to strengthen it and neaten up the edges.

4. Now you can finish the checkerboard mosaic. Cut the scraps of colored paper to size and glue them over the paper design. Use the ideas on pages 9 to 11 to make the border patterns.

5. Make sure all the mosaic pieces are glued down, then carefully fold the paper in half to make a central crease. Align the crease with the center fold of the board and glue in place.

Design a matching box to keep the checkerboard and pieces in.

Try designing other games. Checkers and Ludo are traditional games, but you may like to invent a board game of your own.

SCRIBES AND SCROLLS

THE ROMANS introduced the Latin alphabet to western Europe where it is still used today. However 2,000 years ago, most Romans were illiterate and only the well-educated could read.

The vast Roman administration needed **scribes** to keep records. They wrote on wax tablets, scratching the surface with a **stylus**. It is believed that the speeches of the great Roman emperors and senators were recorded in this way. Permanent records would be transcribed in ink onto **papyrus** scrolls or **vellum**.

The woman above is holding a wax tablet and stylus, and the man has a papyrus scroll. Written scrolls were the Roman equivalent of books.

PAPYRUS SCROLL

YOU WILL NEED

Thick cardboard or foam board	White glue & brush
Ruler & scissors	Papyrus or paper
Mat knife & cutting mat	Paints & brush
Compass & Thumbtacks	Scotch tape
Length of dowel	Cardboard tube & brads
	Scraps of ribbon

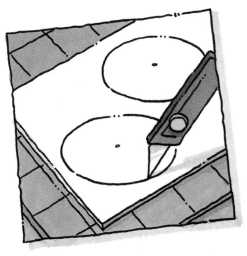

1. Use a compass to draw two 2 1/2 in. (6 cm) circles on the thick cardboard. Then cut the circles out carefully using the mat knife on the cutting mat.

2. Use a compass point to enlarge the center hole in the circles. Attach to each end of the dowel with thumbtacks. Ask an adult to help.

3. Draw two 1 1/2 in. (4 cm) and two 1 in. (2 1/2 cm) circles on the cardboard and cut them out carefully. Glue them onto the larger circle.

4. Wait for the glue to dry, making sure the cardboard circles are firmly secure. Then paint the scroll and decorate the ends with scraps of ribbon.

5. Cut a length of papyrus slightly narrower than the dowel. Write the inscription first before attaching it to the scroll with scotch tape.

6. Make a case for the scroll from a cardboard tube. Paint and decorate it with mosaic patterns (see page 10). Attach a cardboard handle with brads.

Make your scrolls look more authentic by copying a Latin inscription on them.

15

ROMAN TIME

THE **EMPEROR Julius Caesar** organized the Roman calendar into twelve months. We still use this calendar today. Many of the months were named after gods and emperors. January and March were named after the Roman gods **Janus** and Mars. July and August were named after the Emperors **Julius Caesar** and **Augustus**.

The Romans also divided the day into hours. They used letters to represent numbers—I is 1, V is 5, and X is 10. These numerals are still used on some modern clocks and watches.

Circular picture mosaics were often used to decorate walls and pavements. They make perfect designs for a Roman clock face.

MOSAIC CLOCK

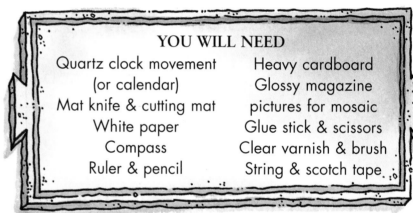

YOU WILL NEED

Quartz clock movement (or calendar) — Heavy cardboard
Mat knife & cutting mat — Glossy magazine pictures for mosaic
White paper — Glue stick & scissors
Compass — Clear varnish & brush
Ruler & pencil — String & scotch tape

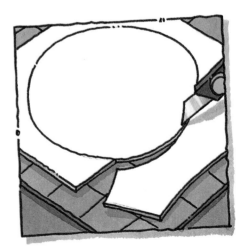

1. The diameter of your clock face will depend on the length of the hands of your quartz movement, but 10 in. (25 cm) is a good size. Draw a 10 in. (25 cm) circle on the paper.

2. Design your clock face using ideas from the mosaic pavement design shown above. Include the numerals in your design and make sure they are correct!

3. Cut out a 10 in. (25 cm) circle from a sheet of heavy cardboard using the mat knife. Transfer the outline of your design onto the cardboard and pencil in the details.

6. Tape a small length of string securely to the back of the mosaic and hang it on the wall.

If you do not have a quartz movement, make the mosaic face and hang a calendar underneath.

4. Cut small mosaic pieces from colored magazine pictures. Choose colors to suit your design. Follow the outlines and glue the pieces in place.

5. Coat the mosaic with clear varnish. This will help to protect the picture. Make a hole in the center and ask an adult to help you install the quartz movement.

The clock face is a circular design with curves, so don't make all the mosaic pieces square.

CLASSIC COLUMNS

THE ROMANS were great architects and engineers, who built on a grand scale. They used columns, arches, vaults, and domes carved from marble and stone to build magnificent **amphitheaters,** temples, **aqueducts,** and bridges. Many are still standing today.

The Romans used columns in the traditional Greek styles, but also developed new types of column tops called capitals, which are still used by architects.

Try making this picture frame with its classical Roman columns. It's impressive enough to frame the portrait of the noble Roman **Emperor** Hadrian!

COLUMN FRAME

1. Draw a 1 1/2 in. (3 1/2 cm) border on cardboard A and cut out the center with a mat knife. Glue 1 1/4 in. (3 cm) wide cardboard strips to three sides of cardboard B. Cover the strips with glue and stick A and B together.

2. Cut lengths of cardboard and glue them to the bottom to make steps. Cut a triangle of cardboard for the roof. Glue it to the top and trim off the extra corners behind.

3. Cut the drinking straws to size and glue them to the sides of the frame to make the columns. Glue the button and the coffee stirrers to the roof to make the decorative frieze.

Paint the columns to look like marble. The tissue paper will give the frame a cracked texture.

4. Tear up small pieces of white tissue and using diluted white glue. Cover the frame with several layers. Make sure the tissue covers all the dents and grooves.

5. Dip lengths of string into the glue and shape them into coils to decorate the tops of the columns. Glue a strip of corrugated cardboard to the roof to look like roof tiles.

6. To make the frame stand up, cut a triangle of cardboard, score and fold it along one side, and glue the fold to the back. Then paint the frame to look like marble.

19

TEMPLES AND SHRINES

THE ROMANS worshiped many different gods and goddesses. Each was associated with a different aspect of life, such as, healing the sick or granting success in battle or business.

Most Roman households had a small shrine where the family could offer prayers and gifts of food or flowers to their favorite gods and goddesses and also remember the spirits of their ancestors.

Snakes were often painted on shrines, such as on this one in the House of Vetii in Italy. The Romans believed that the snake's spirit protected the family.

TEMPLE GIFT BOX

YOU WILL NEED

Two empty cardboard boxes (cereal boxes are ideal)	White glue & brush
Scotch tape	Four cardboard tubes
Scraps of thick cardboard	Corrugated paper
Mat knife & cutting mat	Scissors
Pencil & ruler	Poster paints & brush
	Two brads
	Newspaper

1. Tape over the opening flaps at the top and bottom of both of the empty boxes. Draw a rectangle on the front of one box, 1/2 in. (15 mm) in from the edge, and divide it in half.

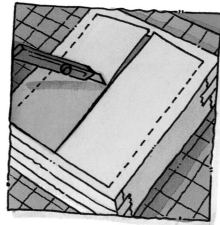

2. The lines show the position of the opening doors. Cut along them carefully with a mat knife. Do not cut along the dotted lines as these will form the door hinges.

3. Cut two pieces of thick cardboard about 2 1/2 in. (6 cm) larger than the base of the box. Glue the box to one of the pieces. The second piece will be used for the roof.

4. Cut the four tubes to the same height as the box and cover them with corrugated paper. Position a tube at each corner of the box, gluing them in place with the white glue.

5. Cut a triangular section from the second box to make a roof that will fit on the second piece of cardboard. Make sure the base of the roof is the same length as the cardboard.

6. Tape the roof shape to the cardboard and glue the roof to the top of the box. Cut a strip of corrugated paper and glue it to the roof. Paint the box and attach the brads to the doors.

Make some shelves or dividers for the gift boxes from strips of cardboard glued into place.

Fill the temple boxes with gifts of candy, stationery, or even soap for a Roman bath!

MARBLE STATUES

GRAND PUBLIC BUILDINGS and temples were built by the Romans to show how important and powerful they were. These structures were filled with huge statues and carved **reliefs** in honor of Roman gods and **emperors**. The Altar of Peace erected by the Emperor **Augustus** in 13 B.C. contains marble statues (left).

Italian quarries provided the sculptors with a plentiful supply of high quality marble. All statues and portraits were extremely realistic, showing every feature and detail with great poise and calm expressions of dignity.

Try casting your own piece of sculpture to use as a handy paperweight!

PLASTER PAPERWEIGHT

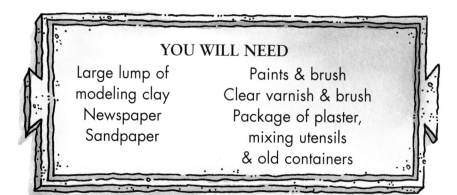

YOU WILL NEED
Large lump of modeling clay
Newspaper
Sandpaper

Paints & brush
Clear varnish & brush
Package of plaster, mixing utensils & old containers

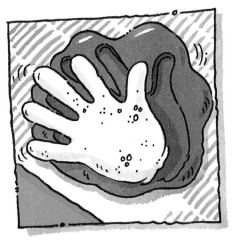

1. Take a large lump of modeling clay and soften it by kneading it with your hands. Press your open hand into the clay, pushing all your fingers in as far as possible.

2. Spread newspaper over the work surface. Using old utensils, mix up the plaster following the instructions on the package. Then pour the plaster into the clay mold.

3. Leave the plaster to set. When it is dry, carefully peel away the clay mold. Parts of the plaster hand may still be slightly damp, so leave it in a safe place to dry out.

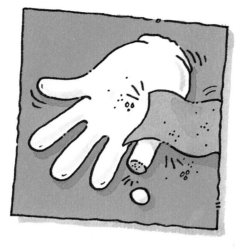 

4. Only when the hand is completely dry can you begin to rub down any unwanted cracks and lumps of plaster with sandpaper.

5. Don't worry if part of a finger breaks off accidentally, or if you lose a thumb—it will just makes the cast look more old and authentic!

6. Finally paint the hand paperweight in the colors of natural marble and leave to dry. Two coats of clear varnish will help to protect it.

Use the hand paperweight to hold paper clips and thumbtacks!

Experiment with making other plaster paperweights. Try taking a plaster cast of your toes!

TERRA-COTTA LAMPS

ROMAN HOMES were lit with oil lamps made from **terra-cotta** or bronze. Each lamp was filled with olive oil and a wick was placed in the nozzle and lit. Because olive oil was expensive people tended to go to bed when it got dark outside.

Some Roman lamps were very elaborate and had several nozzles—many wicks gave a brighter light. Others were beautifully carved by lampmakers with scenes from **mythology** and everyday life. The intricate carvings on the lamps provide us with tiny illustrations of Roman life.

This terra-cotta lamp shows a chariot race at the **Circus Maximus** in Rome (see page 32). It includes details of the spectators, the starting gates, and the chariots.

One example shows details of the harbor at Carthage with fishermen in boats casting their nets. It was made by the lampmaker Augendus in A.D. 200.

CANDLE LAMP

1. Soften the clay in your hands. Then roll it out on a board with a rolling pin until it is about 1/4 in. (1cm) thick. Use a large cookie cutter to cut out a circle of clay.

2. The clay circle will form the base of the lamp. Place the votive candle in the center of the base. Build up the lamp shape around the votive candle with small pieces of clay.

3. Keep adding the clay until it is level with the top of the candle. Use your fingers to flatten the top and shape the sides of the lamp, giving the lamp a curved shape.

YOU WILL NEED

Self-hardening clay   Paints & brush
Wooden carving sticks   Clear varnish
Rolling pin & board   Small sponge
Large cookie cutter   Votive candle

***The lamp is designed to hold a votive candle
It should NOT be lit without an adult's help.**

*The clay lamps can be left
as a natural terra-cotta finish
or painted to look like bronze.*

*These candle lamps are very
pretty, but could become dangerous.
NEVER leave them unattended.*

4. Use a wet sponge to keep the clay damp and to smooth over all the surfaces. Roll out a length of clay into a sausage shape that is long enough to make the handle.

5. Wet the side of the lamp and attach the handle. Curve it into shape and smooth over the joint where it is attached to the side of the lamp. Finally smooth over all the surfaces.

6. Use the wooden sticks to decorate the lamp with a simple pattern. Then leave the lamp in a safe place and let the clay harden before painting and varnishing.

EMPERORS AND RULERS

THE FIRST ROMAN **EMPERORS** refused to wear crowns because they did not want to be thought of as kings, so they wore laurel wreaths. Purple was an expensive dye, so emperors wore **togas** dyed purple as a symbol of their status. It became treason for anyone else to wear a purple toga.

Many modern states have political and legal systems based on the Roman model of government. The American Constitution adopted many Roman ideas, and the words "**senate**" and "republic" are Roman.

This is a bust of the most famous Roman ruler and general, **Julius Caesar**.

YOU WILL NEED

Wide cardboard tube	Newspaper
Corrugated cardboard	Two large bowls
Corrugated paper	White glue & brush
Scissors	Poster paints & brush
Scotch tape	Bay leaves/green paper

IMPERIAL BUST

1. Cut out several squares of corrugated cardboard slightly larger than the diameter of the cardboard tube. Glue them all together and then glue them to the top of the tube with glue.

2. Cut a length of corrugated paper the same width as the tube and use it to cover the tube. Make sure there is enough paper to overlap at the back, then glue it in place.

3. Scrunch up a ball of newspaper until it is large enough for the head. Tape it together firmly. Then secure it to the top of the base with lengths of scotch tape.

5. Press the lumps of pulp to the newspaper head and work all the way round, building up the head shape.

Try making a wreath from bay leaves or green paper to crown the bust.

4. Soak pieces of newspaper in warm water. Then squeeze the water out and mash the paper in another bowl with the white glue to make pulp.

6. Brush on extra glue to help the pulp stick to the head. Add extra pulp and model it with your fingers to shape the features. Take your time to get the head to look right, then allow the pulp to completely dry before painting.

Make a bust of someone you know. Ask them to pose for you. When you have finished, paint the bust to look like stone or marble.

ROMAN COINS

Coins were originally minted in Rome as a method of paying soldiers wages and collecting taxes. During the reign of the **Emperor Augustus,** coins were given a fixed value. Copper coins were worth less than bronze, silver, and gold coins. The same coins were used throughout the Empire to make trading easier.

As the Roman Empire expanded, communication was difficult. Coins were used to spread information and propaganda.

Like the Roman Emperors, try minting your own coins to mark an important event or celebration.

CELEBRATION COIN

YOU WILL NEED

Corrugated cardboard	Scissors & ruler
Paper clip	Paint brush
Modeling clay	Plaster
Board & rolling pin	Newspaper
Old plastic containers	Poster paints in
& mixing utensils	metallic colors

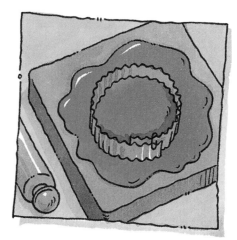

1. Cut a strip of corrugated cardboard and fix it into a circular shape with a paper clip. The strip length will determine the size of the coin.

2. Roll out the modeling clay on a board until it is smooth and flat. Push the corrugated cardboard into the clay, keeping the circular shape.

3. Use old plastic or wooden tools to make patterns and designs in the surface of the clay. These will be the markings on the coin.

4. Follow the instructions on the package to mix up a small amount of plaster. Always use old plastic containers and utensils when making plaster.

5. Pour the plaster into the coin mold to a depth of about 3/4 in. (2 cm). Smooth the surface of the plaster and leave it to dry in a safe place.

6. Remove the plaster coin from the clay mold and peel away the corrugated strip. Now the coin is ready to paint in metallic poster paints.

Make a series of coins and paint them in different metallic paints.

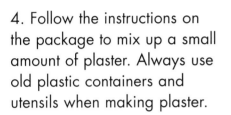

Why not make a blank plaster coin and scratch out a design on the smooth surface using wooden carving tools.

BATTLING GLADIATORS

THE **AMPHITHEATER** was a public arena where performances and games were held. During festivals huge crowds could watch **gladiator** fights, wild beast hunts, and even executions. These events were very violent and thousands of people and animals were killed to entertain the crowds.

Exotic animals, such as lions, panthers, and bears were hunted and brought to the arenas from all parts of the Empire to fight the gladiators.

Gladiators were prisoners and slaves who were trained to fight with all different types of weapons, including swords, **tridents,** and even nets. Some survived, became popular with the crowds, and won their freedom.

GLADIATOR SWORD FIGHT

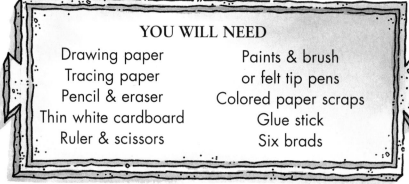

YOU WILL NEED

Drawing paper	Paints & brush
Tracing paper	or felt tip pens
Pencil & eraser	Colored paper scraps
Thin white cardboard	Glue stick
Ruler & scissors	Six brads

1. Make a drawing of two gladiators fighting. Keep the body shapes simple, but draw in all the details of the helmets, shields, and armor.

2. When you are happy with your drawing, trace the top part onto a piece of thin cardboard. Include all the details, except for the legs.

3. Trace the legs onto the cardboard. They will be cut out separately. Make the legs 3/4 in. (2 cm) longer than the drawing.

By holding the main drawing and moving the leg support from side to side the gladiators will appear to fight!

4. Color in your drawing using paints or felt tip pens, or make a collage design with scraps of colored paper glued into place.

5. Carefully cut out the main drawing. Cut close to the lines, but do not worry about cutting around all the small details. Cut out the four legs.

6. Attach the legs to the bodies with brads. Then attach the outer leg of each gladiator to another length of cardboard using brads.

31

CHARIOT RACING

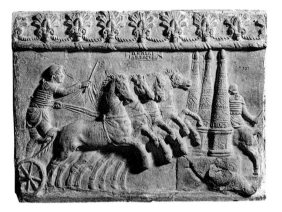

CHARIOT RACING was an exciting occasion that the whole family enjoyed. In Rome the event was held at a huge race track called the **Circus Maximus**. It was an extremely dangerous sport. Chariots were lightweight, built for speed, and usually pulled by a team of four horses called a "quadriga."

A white flag signaled the start then huge starting gates opened and up to twelve chariots raced around the oval track.

There were many fatal accidents, especially on the bends, but victorious **charioteers** became great public heroes.

CHARIOT AND HORSES

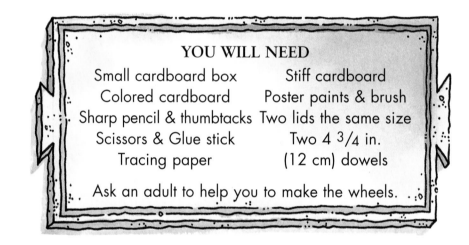

YOU WILL NEED

Small cardboard box · Stiff cardboard
Colored cardboard · Poster paints & brush
Sharp pencil & thumbtacks · Two lids the same size
Scissors & Glue stick · Two 4 3/4 in.
Tracing paper · (12 cm) dowels

Ask an adult to help you to make the wheels.

1. To make the chariot body, take the cardboard box and cut it into a chariot shape (above). Cut off the back and curve the sides and front.

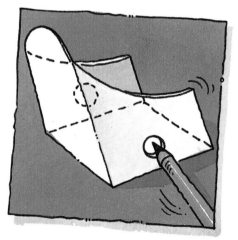

2. Use a sharp pencil to make a hole on both sides of the box. Make sure the two holes line up so the axle for the wheels will thread through.

3. Cut out two circles of cardboard and glue them to the lids. Either paint the chariot body and wheels or decorate them with scraps of colored

4. Draw an outline of a galloping horse on tracing paper. Trace onto cardboard four times and cut them out. Either paint the horses or use different colored cardboard.

5. Carefully push a thumbtack through the center of the lids and attach a lid to one end of the dowel. Pass it through the chariot's body and attach the second lid.

6. Use the sharp pencil to make a hole through the body of each horse. Make sure all the holes line up, then pass the second dowel through all the holes.

7. Cut two strips of cardboard to make reins. Glue one end of each to the chariot and attach the other end to the dowel with a thumbtack.

*Try making several teams of chariots and horses, and race them in your own **Circus Maximus!***

Fill the chariots with candies or small gifts.

WEAPONS OF WAR

THE ROMAN ARMY was a strong, disciplined force led by skilled generals like **Julius Caesar**. Soldiers were well-armed and well-trained, and were supported by teams of craftsmen, who built bridges, weapons, and campsites.

When attacking a heavily defended town, tall siege towers were built near the battle site and pushed into position by teams of men and horses. Huge catapults were made to hurl rocks and burning objects over the walls.

Groups of soldiers in formation used their shields as protection against the enemy.

SIEGE TOWER PERISCOPE

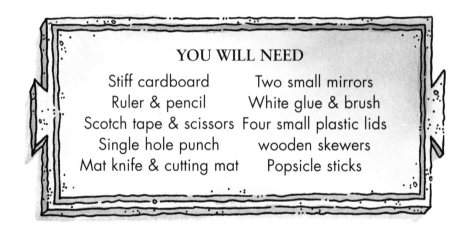

YOU WILL NEED

Stiff cardboard	Two small mirrors
Ruler & pencil	White glue & brush
Scotch tape & scissors	Four small plastic lids
Single hole punch	wooden skewers
Mat knife & cutting mat	Popsicle sticks

1. Cut out a piece of cardboard 11 3/4 in. x 13 1/4 in. (30 cm x 34 cm). Divide it into sections 2 3/4 in. (8 cm) wide, leaving a 3/4 in. (2 cm) flap. Cut two window shapes as shown.

2. Score along the lines. Fold the box and tape it together along the flap edge. Cut out two lengths of cardboard, each 2 3/4 in. x 10 1/4 in.(8 cm x 26 cm). Divide these as shown.

3. Score along the lines. Fold into the triangular shape and tape it together. Glue a mirror to the longest side using the white glue. Then make the second mirror support.

5. Cut out a 4 3/4 in. (12 cm) square of cardboard and cut it into shape shown. Punch two holes in the opposite flaps, making sure the holes line up. Score and fold the flaps and tape them together with scotch tape.

*The shape of the siege tower makes a perfect **periscope** for you to spy on an enemy.*

4. Position a mirror support in the top of the tower. The side of the support should form the top of the box. Tape it in place and position the second mirror in the base.

6. Glue the base to the **periscope.** Ask an adult to make a hole in the center of each lid. Thread a length of skewer through the holes and glue a lid to each end.

Decorate the periscope with pieces of popsicle stick.

Try designing a simple catapult. Make the wheel base, as explained in step 5. Construct the catapult with sections of cardboard, dowel, and an empty bottle cap.

35

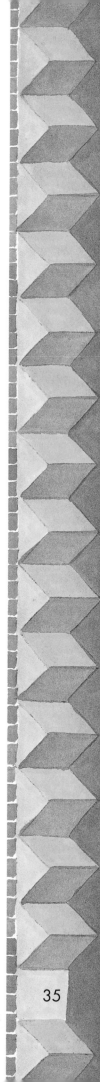

ROMAN RUINS

OVER 1,500 YEARS after the decline of their Empire, the Romans still influence our modern lives. Roman roads were originally built for the army to use, but they soon became vital trade routes, linking major towns by the shortest distances. These routes still service many European cities.

As the Empire expanded, ruling **emperors** wanted to leave their mark. They erected grand buildings and triumphal arches as records of their conquests.

Some Roman buildings are still in use today, however many, like this Roman **Forum** in Italy, are just imposing ruins.

ROMAN RUIN DESK ORGANIZER

YOU WILL NEED

Small cardboard boxes & tubes	Brad
	White glue & brush
Drinking straws	Poster paints & brush
Square cardboard base	Gravel or small stones
White tissue paper	Scotch tape & scissors

1. Gather together the empty cardboard boxes and tubes you have collected and arrange them on the cardboard base. These will become the main parts of the Roman ruin.

2. Cut down the tubes if they are too tall. Then cut the straws to size and glue them to the tubes using white glue. Cover the tubes with glued pieces of white tissue paper.

3. If you have a small empty box with a sliding drawer, make a handle in the drawer with a brad. This will become a handy pencil or pen drawer.

4. Cut the lids off some of the small boxes and tape the sides together so they don't fall apart. Now stack up the boxes and arrange all the pieces again on the base.

5. When you are happy with the arrangement, glue all the pieces together with white glue. Cover the boxes with glued pieces of tissue and glue small stones to the base.

6. When the glue has dried, paint the ruined columns and masonry to look like marble. Don't forget to paint some cracks in the columns to make them look old.

This Roman ruin makes an impressive desk organizer.

GLOSSARY

Amphitheater – a large arena with tiered seats so that thousands of spectators can watch the games

Aqueducts – water channels, often raised above ground, that supplied a city with water

Asia Minor a large area of land that formed the eastern extent of the Roman Empire, know today as Turkey and Syria

Augustus – the first emperor of Rome, who ruled between 27 B.C. and A.D. 14

Charioteer – a chariot driver, usually a slave. Successful charioteers, like **gladiators**, became popular with the crowds and sometimes made enough profit to buy their freedom

Circus – a large sports arena used for athletic contests and chariot racing

Circus Maximus – a huge race track in the center of Rome

built for chariot racing. It had seating for 45,000 spectators and underground cages for wild animals. The main arena could be flooded to stage sea battles

Colosseum – the large **amphitheater** in the center of Rome built for **gladiator** fights

Emperor – the ruler of Rome, who had great power over the army and the senate

Etruscans – a race of people who lived in central Italy in Roman times

Forum – the central market square of a city, often paved, and surrounded by important public buildings

Gaul – the ancient name for the area known today as France

Gladiators – slaves or prisoners that were trained to fight in the **amphitheater** arenas